Microwave Party Cooking

Written by
Barbara Bloch

Illustrated by
Ellen Witteborg and
Sandra Baenen

PETER PAUPER PRESS, INC.
WHITE PLAINS • NEW YORK

TABLE OF CONTENTS

INTRODUCTION

Company coming? Now that you have a microwave oven you can entertain more easily than ever before. Use your oven to make the recipes that follow, and use it to reheat food at the last minute instead of keeping food warm in a conventional oven where it may dry out. When company is late, or lingers over cocktails longer than you expected, you don't have to worry about serving cold food.

A few words of caution:

All the recipes in this book were tested in a 650 watt oven. If the wattage of your oven is higher or lower, you will have to adjust cooking times by a few minutes. Undercook and check; you can always add a few minutes, but you can't fix overcooked food.

Undercook food slightly if you plan to reheat it. And bring it to room temperature before reheating.

Remember that microwave cooking is moist cooking. Don't use the microwave to reheat food that is supposed to be nice and crisp.

In these recipes, "cover loosely" means to use microproof plastic wrap vented at one corner.

Don't forget that the amount of time necessary to cook or reheat food in a microwave oven is directly affected by the temperature of the food and the amount of food placed in the oven.

Now, you're ready for microwave party cooking!

B. B.

Appetizers and First Courses

STUFFED MUSHROOMS

20 large mushrooms
6   tablespoons butter, divided
3   shallots, finely chopped
½   cup dry bread crumbs
3   tablespoons chopped fresh parsley
1   tablespoon snipped dill
¼   cup dry sherry
1   tablespoon lemon juice
    Salt and freshly ground pepper to taste
    Paprika
    Tiny parsley sprigs to garnish

Wipe mushrooms with damp cloth and remove stems. Set mushroom caps aside and mince stems. Place 3 tablespoons butter in 2-quart microproof dish and microcook on high 1 minute or until melted. Add minced stems and shallots, cover loosely, and microcook on high 3 minutes. Stir in bread crumbs, parsley, dill, sherry, lemon juice, salt, and pepper, and set aside. Place remaining 3 tablespoons butter in 1-cup glass measure and microcook on high 1 minute or until melted. Brush mushroom caps with melted butter and fill mushrooms with stuffing. Arrange 12 mushrooms, stuffing side up, in 10-inch

6

microproof pie plate and sprinkle with paprika. Microcook on high 5 minutes. Repeat with remaining mushrooms. Garnish each mushroom with tiny parsley sprig and serve hot.

20 appetizers

SPICY SHRIMP APPETIZERS

20 slices bacon (about 1 pound)
40 medium-size shrimp, (about 1½ pounds), peeled and deveined, with tails left on
¾ cup plum or duck sauce
½ cup dry vermouth
½ cup soy sauce
⅓ cup honey
1 tablespoon minced garlic
1 tablespoon Dijon-style mustard
1 tablespoon ground ginger

Place 5 bacon slices in single layer on microproof rack. Cover with paper towels and microcook on high about 2½ minutes or until bacon is partially cooked. Remove from rack and place on paper towels to drain. Drain fat from rack and repeat 3 times with remaining bacon slices. Cut slices in half. Wrap half piece of bacon around each shrimp and secure

7

with wooden toothpicks. Arrange wrapped
shrimp in circular pattern, tails toward
center, in two 10-inch microproof pie
plates or round dishes with rim.
Combine plum sauce, vermouth, soy
sauce, honey, garlic, mustard, and ginger
in bowl and stir until well blended. Pour
marinade over shrimp and turn shrimp to
coat on all sides. Cover with plastic wrap
and refrigerate several hours or overnight.
Replace plastic wrap with paper towels
and microcook 1 plate of shrimp on high
about 5 minutes or until shrimp are
cooked. Repeat with second plate of
shrimp. Arrange shrimp on serving plate.
Pour marinade into small bowl and serve
as dipping sauce.

40 appetizers

SHERRIED BLACK BEAN SOUP

1	package (16 ounces) dried black beans
6	slices bacon, diced
2	onions, chopped
3	cloves garlic, crushed
1	stalk celery, chopped
1	tablespoon chili powder
1	teaspoon cumin

1	teaspoon ground cloves
	Salt and freshly ground pepper to taste
9-11	cups hot chicken stock or chicken broth, divided
½	cup dry sherry
	Lemon slices to garnish
	Chopped scallions, finely chopped hard-cooked egg, and dairy sour cream to serve

Rinse beans and pick over carefully. Pour 6 cups hot water into 3-quart microproof casserole, add beans, cover, and micro-cook on high 20 minutes. Set aside and let stand, covered, 1½ hours. Place diced bacon in 5-quart microproof casserole. Cover and microcook on high 4 minutes, stirring once. Stir in onions, garlic, and celery. Re-cover and microcook on high 8 minutes, stirring once. Drain beans and discard liquid. Add beans to casserole and stir in chili powder, cumin, cloves, salt, and pepper. Add 6 cups hot stock and stir. Cover and microcook on high 1 hour, stirring every 20 minutes. Add remaining 3 cups hot stock, re-cover, and microcook on high 1 hour, or until beans are tender, stirring every 20 minutes. Add additional liquid, if necessary. Measure half of soup and pour into container of

food processor or blender in batches.
Process until puréed. Combine with
remaining soup and reheat, if necessary.
Stir in sherry. Ladle into bowls and
garnish each serving with lemon slice.
Serve with chopped scallions, chopped
egg, and sour cream.

6 servings

GLAZED CHICKEN DRUMMETTES

⅓   cup soy sauce
2   tablespoons honey
2   tablespoons ketchup
2   tablespoons dry sherry
1   teaspoon dry mustard
1   clove garlic, minced
16   chicken drummettes

Combine soy sauce, honey, ketchup,
sherry, mustard, and garlic in bowl and
stir until well blended. Arrange drummettes in single layer in shallow glass
baking dish. Pour soy sauce mixture over
and turn drummettes to coat. Cover and
refrigerate several hours or overnight,
turning occasionally. Arrange drummettes
in 10-inch microproof pie plate, spoke-

fashion, with thickest part at outer edge
of plate. Cover loosely with plastic wrap
and microcook on high 10 minutes,
turning drummettes over after 5 minutes.
Remove drummettes to serving dish.
Pour marinade into serving bowl and
serve as dipping sauce.

16 appetizers

Note: A drummette is the large part of a
chicken wing. This recipe will also work
well with 8 whole chicken wings, cut in
half, tips removed.

HOT CRAB DIP

1   can (6 ounces) crab meat
1   package (8 ounces) cream cheese,
    softened
3   tablespoons mayonnaise
2   tablespoons snipped chives
1   tablespoon Worcestershire sauce
1   teaspoon lemon juice
    Hot pepper sauce to taste
    Paprika to garnish
    Melba rounds or crackers to serve

Drain crab meat, pick over, and set aside.

Combine cream cheese, mayonnaise, chives, Worcestershire, lemon juice, and hot pepper sauce in bowl. Stir until thoroughly blended. Add reserved crab meat and stir. Spoon mixture into small microproof serving dish. Cover loosely and microcook at 50% power 2½ minutes. Stir well and smooth top. Re-cover and microcook at 50% power 2½ minutes or until hot and bubbly. Sprinkle with paprika and serve with melba rounds or crackers.

About 2 cups

CHILI-CHEDDAR CANAPES

1½ cups (6 ounces) shredded Cheddar
       cheese
6   tablespoons butter, softened
1   can (4 ounces) green chili peppers,
       drained and finely chopped
2   medium-size onions, finely chopped
1   large clove garlic, crushed
¼   cup mayonnaise
1   teaspoon Worcestershire sauce
       Hot pepper sauce to taste
26   melba rounds
       Chopped parsley to garnish

Place all ingredients except melba rounds and parsley in medium-size bowl. Stir until thoroughly combined. Spread mixture on melba rounds. Place in single layer on round microproof plates. Microcook 1 plate of melba rounds at a time at 50% power 2 to 3 minutes, or until cheese is melted. Repeat with remaining plates of melba rounds. Garnish with parsley and serve hot.

26 appetizers

CHOPPED CHICKEN LIVERS MADEIRA

1 pound chicken livers
2 tablespoons chicken fat or butter
1 large onion, finely chopped
2 cloves garlic, minced
   Salt and freshly ground pepper to taste
2 hard-cooked eggs, coarsely chopped
2 tablespoons Madeira
1 tablespoon mayonnaise
   Cocktail bread to serve

Rinse chicken livers, pat dry, and cut in half. Trim off excess fat. Place chicken fat in 1-quart shallow microproof dish and microcook on high 1 minute or until melted. Add chicken livers, onion, garlic, salt, and pepper. Stir well, cover loosely, and microcook on high 7 minutes or until chicken livers are no longer pink inside, stirring every 2½ minutes. Spoon into container of food processor or blender. Add eggs, Madeira, and mayonnaise, and process but do not purée. Spoon into serving bowl and refrigerate several hours. Serve with cocktail bread.

About 2 cups

HAM CLOUDS

1	can (6¾ ounces) chunked ham, mashed
⅓	cup Russian dressing
2	tablespoons minced onion
1	package (3 ounces) cream cheese, softened
1	egg yolk
1	teaspoon baking powder
	Hot pepper sauce to taste
36	melba rounds
	Paprika

Place ham, dressing, and onion in small bowl and stir well. Combine cream cheese, egg yolk, baking powder, and hot pepper sauce in small bowl and stir until smooth. Spoon ham mixture onto melba rounds. Spread cream cheese mixture on top of ham mixture and sprinkle with paprika. Place in single layer on round microproof plates. Microcook 1 plate of melba rounds at a time at 50% power 2 to 3 minutes, or until cheese is melted. Repeat with remaining plates of melba rounds and serve hot.

36 appetizers

VICHYSSOISE

3 tablespoons butter
4 cups peeled, cubed potatoes
2 cups thinly sliced leeks
4 cups chicken stock, divided
   Salt and freshly ground white pepper
   to taste
1 cup heavy cream
   Snipped fresh chives to garnish

Place butter in 3-quart microproof casserole and microcook on high 1 minute or until melted. Add potatoes and leeks. Stir well, cover, and microcook on high about 15 minutes or until vegetables are tender, stirring once. Spoon mixture into container of food processor or blender, add 1½ cups stock and process until smooth. Return mixture to casserole. Add remaining 2½ cups stock, salt, and pepper. Stir well, cover, and microcook on high 8 minutes. Stir in cream and set aside to cool. When cool, refrigerate until thoroughly chilled. Ladle into small bowls, garnish with chives, and serve cold.

6 servings

Note: If soup is thicker than desired, stir in additional cream.

The Main Course

BROILED SHAD ROE

2 pair shad roe
2 tablespoons lemon juice
   Chervil
   Salt and freshly ground pepper to taste
   Butter
4 slices bacon
   Lemon wedges to serve
   Melted butter to serve (optional)

Rinse shad roe and prick gently in several places with fork. Place in single layer in microproof baking dish. Add just enough water to cover and stir lemon juice into water. Cover loosely and microcook on high 6 to 8 minutes or until shad roe are no longer pink. Transfer carefully to broiler pan. Sprinkle with chervil, salt, and pepper. Dot with butter and broil in conventional oven or broiler 3 to 4 minutes. Turn over carefully, season, and dot with butter. Broil 3 to 4 minutes. Place bacon on microproof rack. Cover with paper towels and microcook on high about 4 minutes or until bacon is crisp. Drain on paper towels. Place bacon on top of shad roe and serve with lemon wedges and melted butter, if desired.

4 servings

SHRIMP CREOLE

1   tablespoon cornstarch
2   cans (16 ounces each) stewed tomatoes
2   slices bacon, cooked and crumbled
1   onion, chopped
2   stalks celery, chopped
1   clove garlic, minced
1   tablespoon chopped fresh parsley
1   tablespoon Dijon-style mustard
1   teaspoon chili powder
¼   teaspoon cayenne
    Salt and freshly ground pepper to taste
1   pound medium-size shrimp, peeled
    and deveined
    Hot cooked rice to serve

Stir cornstarch into small amount of
liquid from stewed tomatoes until
smooth. Add to remainder of stewed
tomatoes. Place in 2-quart microproof
casserole. Add bacon, onion, celery,
garlic, parsley, mustard, chili powder,
cayenne, salt, and pepper. Stir well.
Cover and microcook on high 6 minutes,
stirring once. Stir in shrimp, cover, and
microcook on high 3 to 4 minutes or
until shrimp are cooked. Serve over hot
cooked rice.

4 servings

SAUCY FLOUNDER

4 small flounder fillets (about 1 pound)
   Salt and freshly ground pepper to taste
3 tablespoons lemon juice, divided
2 tablespoons seasoned bread crumbs
2 tablespoons grated Parmesan cheese
1 tablespoon chopped fresh parsley
½ teaspoon tarragon
2 tablespoons half-and-half
½ cup dairy sour cream
   Paprika

Rinse fish under cold water and pat dry.
Arrange in single layer in microproof
baking dish, placing thickest part of fish
at outer edge of dish. Season with salt
and pepper and sprinkle with 2
tablespoons lemon juice. Cover loosely
and microcook on high 3 minutes.
Combine bread crumbs, cheese, parsley,
and tarragon in small bowl. Add half-and-
half, sour cream, and remaining tablespoon lemon juice. Stir well. Drain liquid
from fish and stir into sour cream
mixture. Spread evenly over fillets and
sprinkle with paprika. Microcook at 50%
power about 4 minutes or until fish
flakes easily.

4 servings

CURRIED TURKEY CASSEROLE

3   tablespoons butter
1   large onion, chopped
½   cup chopped celery
2½ tablespoons all-purpose flour
1   tablespoon curry powder
⅛   teaspoon ground clove
2   cups chicken broth
2   tablespoons lemon juice
3   cups cubed cooked turkey
1   tart apple, peeled and chopped
½   cup snipped pitted prunes
    Salt and freshly ground pepper to taste
    Hot cooked rice to serve

Place butter, onion, and celery in 2½-quart microproof casserole and stir. Cover and microcook on high 4 minutes. Stir flour, curry powder, clove, chicken broth, and lemon juice until blended. Add to onion mixture. Cover and microcook on high 5 minutes, stirring once. Add turkey, apple, prunes, salt, and pepper. Stir well, re-cover, and microcook on high 12 to 13 minutes, stirring every 4 minutes. Serve over hot cooked rice.

4 servings

CRISP DUCK WITH
RASPBERRY SAUCE

1 4½ to 5 pound duckling
   Salt and freshly ground pepper
1 tart apple, quartered and cored
1 stalk celery, cut into large chunks
1 medium-size onion, quartered
2-3 parsley sprigs

Raspberry Sauce:

1 package (10 ounces) frozen raspberries
¼ cup sugar
1 tablespoon plus 1 teaspoon cornstarch
½ cup dry vermouth
1 tablespoon lemon juice
¼ cup red currant jelly
2 tablespoons Framboise or brandy
1 cup fresh raspberries (optional) and
   parsley sprigs to garnish

Remove giblets and discard or set aside
to use another time. Rinse duck and pat
dry with paper towels. Remove excess fat
and season duck inside and outside with
salt and pepper. Secure neck skin to back
with wooden toothpicks. Place apple,
celery, onion, and parsley in cavity of
duck and tie legs together with kitchen
string. Prick duck all over and place,
breast side down, on microproof rack set
in microproof roasting pan. Cover loosely

with waxed paper and microcook at 70% power 18 minutes. Drain off fat. Turn duck over, re-cover, and microcook at 70% power 14 to 16 minutes, or until instant meat thermometer inserted between leg and thigh registers 180° F. Preheat broiler in conventional oven. Cut duck into quarters and place, skin side up, on metal rack in metal broiler pan. Broil 6 to 8 minutes or until skin is crisp and well browned. Keep duck warm until ready to serve. Place package of frozen raspberries on microproof plate. Pierce package and microcook on high 2 minutes to thaw. Drain thawed raspberries and reserve syrup. Mash berries gently and set aside. Place sugar and cornstarch in 4-cup glass measure and stir to combine. Add reserved raspberry syrup and vermouth and stir until smooth. Add lemon juice and jelly and stir well. Microcook on high 3 minutes 30 seconds, stirring once. Stir in mashed raspberries and Framboise. Microcook on high 2 minutes 45 seconds, or until sauce is thickened, stirring once. Place duck on warm serving dish and spoon a little hot sauce over. Garnish with fresh raspberries and sprigs of parsley. Pour remaining sauce into bowl and pass separately.

4 servings

VEAL CASSEROLE

1½ pounds veal for stew, cut into
    1½-inch cubes
    Salt and freshly ground pepper to taste
3 tablespoons all-purpose flour
3 tablespoons vegetable oil
4 medium-size carrots, peeled and
    thickly sliced
12 pearl onions
2 cups chicken broth
1 can (6 ounces) tomato paste
⅓ cup Dijon-style mustard
1 large clove garlic, minced
½ teaspoon Italian seasoning
1 package (10 ounces) frozen tiny
    peas, thawed
    Hot cooked noodles to serve
    Chopped fresh parsley to garnish

Season veal with salt and pepper and
dredge lightly in flour. Shake off excess
flour. Heat oil in skillet, add meat, and
cook until browned on all sides. Remove
meat from skillet with slotted spoon and
place in 3-quart microproof casserole.
Add carrots and onions. Blend chicken
broth, tomato paste, mustard, garlic, and
Italian seasoning in medium-size bowl.
Pour over meat and stir well. Cover and
microcook on high 10 minutes. Stir, re-

24

cover, and microcook at 50% power 45 minutes, stirring twice during cooking. Stir in peas, re-cover, and microcook at 50% power 5 minutes. Serve over hot cooked noodles and garnish with parsley.

6 servings

STIFADO

1½ pounds boneless beef chuck, cut
    into 1-inch cubes
    Salt and freshly ground pepper to taste
4   tablespoons butter
1   large clove garlic, crushed
2   medium-size onions, sliced
½   cup beef broth
5   tablespoons tomato paste
¼   cup dry red wine
1   tablespoon red wine vinegar
1   tablespoon brown sugar
¼   teaspoon cumin
⅛   teaspoon ground clove
2   tablespoons raisins (optional)
1   bay leaf
1   cinnamon stick
    Hot cooked noodles to serve

Trim excess fat from meat and season with salt and pepper. Set aside. Place

butter in 2-quart microproof casserole
and microcook on high 1 minute. Add
garlic, cover loosely, and microcook on
high 1 minute. Add beef cubes and stir
until well coated. Cover with sliced
onions. Combine beef broth, tomato
paste, wine, vinegar, sugar, cumin, clove,
and raisins in small bowl. Mix well and
spoon over meat and onions. Add bay leaf
and cinnamon stick and push down
under meat. Cover and microcook on
high 8 minutes, stirring once. Reduce
power to 50%, re-cover, and microcook
50 to 55 minutes, or until beef is tender,
stirring every 20 minutes. Remove bay
leaf and cinnamon stick. Serve over hot
cooked noodles.

4 servings

LAMB-STUFFED EGGPLANT

1   large eggplant
¾   pound lean ground lamb
1   medium-size onion, chopped
2   cloves garlic, minced
1   medium-size tomato, chopped
1   egg, lightly beaten
½   teaspoon cinnamon

¼   teaspoon nutmeg
¼   teaspoon cumin
    Salt and freshly ground pepper to taste
2   cups (8 ounces) shredded mozzarella,
    divided

Trim ends of eggplant and cut in half
lengthwise. Cook in lightly salted boiling
water 8 to 10 minutes. Drain well and set
aside until cool enough to handle.
Hollow out eggplant halves, leaving ½-
inch thick shell. Discard seeds, chop
pulp, and set aside. Place lamb, onion,
garlic, and tomato in medium-size
microproof bowl. Stir well, cover loosely,
and microcook on high 5 minutes,
stirring once. Drain off fat. Add reserved
eggplant pulp, egg, cinnamon, nutmeg,
cumin, salt, pepper, and 1 cup mozzarella.
Mix well and spoon into eggplant shells.
Place shells, filled side up, side by side in
microproof baking dish. Cover loosely
and microcook on high 3 minutes. Rotate
dish ¼ turn, decrease power to 50%, and
microcook 8 minutes. Sprinkle with
remaining 1 cup mozzarella and microcook at 50% power 1½ to 2 minutes, or
until cheese is melted.

4 servings

HOT TEXAS CHILI

1   pound Italian bulk sausage
1   pound lean ground beef
3   tablespoons olive oil
2   cloves garlic, minced
2   large onions, sliced
1   can (28 ounces) whole peeled tomatoes, chopped
1   can (16 ounces) red kidney beans
2   tablespoons chili powder, or to taste
1   teaspoon cumin
1   teaspoon crushed hot red pepper or crushed jalapeño pepper (optional)
    Salt and freshly ground pepper to taste
    Hot cooked spaghetti or rice, grated sharp Cheddar cheese and finely chopped onion to serve

Place sausage and ground beef in 2-quart microproof casserole. Cover loosely and microcook on high 6 to 8 minutes, or until meat loses pink color, stirring every 2 minutes. Drain off excess fat and place meat in large bowl. Wipe out casserole with paper towel. Place oil, garlic, and onions in casserole and stir. Cover loosely and microcook on high 3 minutes. Add to meat. Add tomatoes with their liquid, undrained beans, chili powder, cumin, crushed red pepper, salt,

28

and pepper to meat and stir until well
combined. Divide mixture in half and
place in two 2-quart microproof casseroles. Cover 1 casserole and microcook
on high 16 to 18 minutes, stirring twice.
Repeat with second casserole. Serve over
hot cooked spaghetti or rice and top
with Cheddar cheese and chopped
onion.

2 casseroles, 6 servings each

Note: If desired, set 1 casserole aside
until cool, cover, and freeze for use
another time. Defrost in microwave oven
at 30% power. Reheat at 70% power,
stirring several times.

BAKED SCALLOPS

1   pound bay scallops
3   tablespoons butter
3   scallions, thinly sliced
1   tablespoon lemon or lime juice
1   tablespoon freshly chopped parsley
½   teaspoon basil
     Salt and freshly ground pepper to taste
     Chopped fresh parsley to garnish

Rinse scallops under cold water. Drain
well, place on paper towel and pat dry.

Set aside. Place butter in microproof pie plate. Microcook on high 1 minute or until melted. Add scallions, lemon juice, parsley, basil, salt, and pepper. Stir well. Add scallops and toss lightly to coat. Cover loosely and microcook at 50% power 4 minutes or until tender. (Do not overcook.) Spoon into serving dish and garnish with chopped parsley.

4 servings

STUFFED RAINBOW TROUT

4   rainbow trout (about ¾ pound each)
2   tablespoons butter, melted
1½ tablespoons lemon juice
¼   teaspoon paprika

Stuffing:

6   tablespoons butter
1   medium-size onion, chopped
1   cup chopped mushrooms
½   cup chopped celery
¼   cup chopped green pepper
    Salt and freshly ground pepper to taste
1   cup herbed stuffing mix
    Dill sprigs and lemon wedges to garnish

30

Grease microproof baking dish and set aside. Rinse fish under cold water, pat dry, and set aside. Combine 2 tablespoons melted butter, lemon juice, and paprika and set aside. To prepare stuffing, place 6 tablespoons butter in medium-size microproof bowl and microcook on high 1 minute or until melted. Add onion, mushrooms, celery, green pepper, salt, and pepper. Cover loosely and microcook on high 4 minutes. Add stuffing mix and toss until well combined. Fill cavities of fish and tie fish securely with kitchen string to keep stuffing in place. Place fish in prepared baking dish with thickest part at outer edge of dish. Brush skin liberally on both sides with half of reserved butter-lemon mixture. Cover loosely with waxed paper and microcook on high 5 minutes. Turn fish over and brush with remaining butter-lemon mixture. Re-cover and microcook on high 5 minutes, or until fish flakes easily. Serve garnished with dill sprigs and lemon wedges.

4 servings

CHICKEN SALAD À LA GRECQUE

1   English cucumber
2   tablespoons lemon juice, divided
1½ pounds chicken cutlets, cut into
      1-inch cubes
1   teaspoon sweet paprika
      Salt and freshly ground pepper to taste
1   red pepper, seeded and chopped
1   medium-size onion, thinly sliced

Dressing:

6   tablespoons olive oil
5   tablespoons lemon juice
1   large clove garlic, minced
1   tablespoon freshly chopped parsley
      Salt and freshly ground pepper to taste

To Serve:

      Romaine lettuce
1   large tomato, cut into wedges
½   cup crumbled feta cheese
      Greek olives

Peel cucumber and cut into sticks about
1½ x ¼ inches. Place in 2-quart
microproof casserole and sprinkle with 1

tablespoon lemon juice. Cover and microcook on high 4 minutes, stirring once. Transfer to bowl with slotted spoon and set aside to cool. Place chicken in casserole and sprinkle with paprika, salt, pepper, and remaining tablespoon lemon juice. Stir to coat. Cover and microcook on high 6 minutes or until chicken is no longer pink, stirring once. Remove with slotted spoon, place in large bowl, and set aside to cool. Add red pepper and onion to chicken and toss lightly. To make dressing, combine oil, lemon juice, garlic, parsley, salt, and pepper in screw-top jar and shake well. Spoon 1 tablespoon dressing over reserved cucumbers and stir to coat. Cover and refrigerate until well chilled. Pour remaining dressing over chicken mixture. Stir well, cover, and refrigerate until chilled. To serve, line salad bowl with romaine lettuce. Spoon chicken mixture into center of bowl and arrange cucumber sticks and tomato wedges around edge. Sprinkle feta cheese over salad and top with olives.

6 servings

POACHED SOLE WITH DILL SAUCE

4   small sole fillets (about 1 pound)
    Salt and freshly ground pepper to taste
1   onion, thinly sliced
3   tablespoons chopped fresh dill, divided
¼   cup dry white wine or vermouth
1   tablespoon butter
1   tablespoon all-purpose flour
    Light cream or milk
    Dill sprigs to garnish

Rinse fish under cold water and pat dry.
Arrange in single layer in microproof
baking dish, placing thickest part of fish
at outer edge of dish. Season with salt
and pepper. Arrange onion rings on top
of fish, sprinkle with 1½ tablespoons dill,
and pour wine over. Cover loosely with
waxed paper and microcook on high 6
minutes or until fish flakes easily. Remove
fish to serving dish with slotted spatula
and keep warm, reserving liquid. Place
butter in 2-cup glass measure and
microcook on high 1 minute or until
melted. Stir flour into butter and
microcook on high 1 minute. Pour
cooking liquid into glass measure slowly,
stirring. Add enough cream to make 1
cup. Season with salt and pepper and
microcook on high 1 minute or until

sauce is thickened. Add additional cream or wine, if desired. Stir in remaining 1½ tablespoons dill. Pour over fish and garnish with sprigs of dill.

4 servings

QUICK PICNIC CHICKEN

2   broiler/fryer chickens (about 4 pounds each), split or quartered
    Barbecue sauce (homemade or prepared)

Rinse chicken under cold water and pat dry. Place 1 chicken on microproof broiler rack, cover loosely with waxed paper, and microcook on high 6 minutes. Turn chicken over and microcook on high 6 minutes. Set chicken aside and repeat with second chicken. Brush chicken with barbecue sauce and finish cooking on grill or broil in conventional oven or broiler about 4 minutes on each side or just until crisp.

6 servings

Note: Chicken may be microcooked ahead of time, refrigerated, and finished quickly on grill or under broiler just before serving.

Vegetables and Much More

BOURBON SWEET POTATOES

2   cans (23 ounces each) whole
    sweet potatoes
3   tablespoons butter
¼   cup orange juice
¼   cup bourbon
2   tablespoons brown sugar
¼   teaspoon cinnamon
¼   teaspoon nutmeg
⅛   teaspoon ground clove
    Salt and freshly ground pepper to taste
⅓   cup chopped pecans to garnish

Drain sweet potatoes and arrange in
single layer in baking dish. Place butter in
2-cup glass measure. Cover loosely and
microcook on high 1½ minutes or until
melted. Stir in orange juice, bourbon,
brown sugar, cinnamon, nutmeg, clove,
salt, and pepper. Re-cover and microcook
on high 1 minute. Pour over potatoes and
turn potatoes to coat on all sides. Cover
loosely and microcook on high 3
minutes. Baste potatoes with sauce, re-
cover, and microcook at 50% power 3 to
4 minutes or until heated through.
Garnish with pecans.

8 servings

SPINACH-STUFFED TOMATOES

6   firm tomatoes
1   package (10 ounces) frozen chopped
    spinach
3   tablespoons butter
1   onion, diced
¼   pound mushrooms, chopped
2   eggs, beaten
¾   cup grated Parmesan cheese, divided
½   cup crushed herbed stuffing mix
3   tablespoons slivered almonds
1   teaspoon basil
    Salt and freshly ground pepper to taste

Cut slice off tops of tomatoes and
remove cores. Scoop out pulp leaving ½-
inch shells. Sprinkle inside of tomatoes
with salt, invert on paper towels, and let
stand 30 minutes. Place frozen spinach in
bowl and microcook on high 5 minutes
or until completely thawed. Squeeze dry
and set aside. Place butter in 1½-quart
microproof casserole and microcook on
high 1 minute or until melted. Add onion
and mushrooms. Cover and microcook
on high 2 minutes. Stir in spinach, eggs,
½ cup cheese, stuffing mix, almonds,
basil, salt, and pepper. Spoon into
tomatoes and arrange tomatoes in circle

in 9-inch microproof pie plate. Microcook
on high 6 minutes, rotating plate once.
Sprinkle with remaining ¼ cup cheese
and microcook on high 1 minute.

6 servings

HOT GERMAN POTATO SALAD

6   medium-size potatoes, peeled and sliced
1   medium-size onion, chopped
6   slices bacon
2   tablespoons all-purpose flour
1   tablespoon sugar
1   teaspoon celery seed
    Salt and freshly-ground pepper to taste
1   teaspoon Dijon-style mustard
6   tablespoons cider vinegar
    Paprika and chopped fresh parsley
    to garnish

Place 1 cup lightly salted water in 2-quart
microproof casserole. Add potatoes and
onion. Microcook on high 12 minutes or
just until tender. Drain and set aside.
Place bacon on microproof rack, cover
with paper towels, and microcook on
high 5 minutes or until crisp. Drain on
paper towels, reserving 3 tablespoons
drippings. Place reserved drippings (or

substitute 3 tablespoons melted butter),
flour, sugar, celery seed, salt, and pepper
in 4-cup glass measure and stir well.
Microcook on high 1 minute. Stir in
mustard, vinegar, and ¾ cup water.
Microcook on high 3 to 4 minutes or
until mixture thickens and comes to a
boil, stirring once. Crumble bacon and
sprinkle over potatoes. Pour hot dressing
over and toss gently to coat. Adjust
seasoning. Cover loosely and microcook
on high 4 minutes or until heated
through. Garnish with paprika and
parsley.

6 servings

APPLE-STUFFED ACORN SQUASH

2   tablespoons chopped raisins
1   tablespoon Calvados
2   medium-size acorn squash
1   large apple, peeled and diced
3   tablespoons brown sugar
⅓   cup chopped walnuts
½   teaspoon cinnamon
¼   teaspoon nutmeg
4   tablespoons melted butter, divided
    Salt and freshly ground pepper to taste

Place raisins in small bowl and pour
Calvados over. Set aside. Pierce squash
several times with fork, pushing fork into
center of squash to prevent it from
bursting. Place squash on microproof
rack and microcook on high 12 minutes.
Set aside until cool enough to handle.
Combine apple, brown sugar, walnuts,
cinnamon, nutmeg, reserved raisins, and
2 tablespoons melted butter in bowl and
stir to combine. Cut squash in half
lengthwise and scoop out centers. Brush
cut edges and cavities of squash with
remaining 2 tablespoons melted butter.
Season with salt and pepper and fill with
apple mixture. Place, filled side up, in
shallow microproof casserole. Cover
loosely and microcook on high 10
minutes, or until squash are tender.

4 servings

SPICY BEETS

8   medium-size beets, uniform in size
1   tablespoon butter
3   tablespoons creamy horseradish sauce
3   tablespoons light cream
2   teaspoons prepared horseradish
    Salt and freshly ground pepper to taste

Scrub and trim beets, leaving bottom ends and about 1½ inches on tops to prevent "bleeding." Place in microproof casserole, add 1 cup water, cover, and microcook on high about 20 minutes or until beets are tender, turning beets over with spoon and rearranging every 5 minutes. Drain and set aside to cool. Place butter in casserole and microcook on high 30 seconds or until melted. Add horseradish sauce, cream, prepared horseradish, salt, and pepper. Stir well. Peel and slice reserved beets. Add to sauce and turn to coat. Cover and microcook on high 1½ to 2 minutes or until heated through.

4 servings

EGGPLANT-SQUASH CASSEROLE

¼ cup olive oil
1 eggplant (about 1 pound), peeled and cubed
1 large onion, sliced
2 cloves garlic, thinly sliced
1 summer squash (about 1 pound), thinly sliced
1 green pepper, seeded and cut into strips

1   can (16 ounces) peeled tomatoes,
    chopped
2   tablespoons chopped fresh parsley
½   teaspoon basil
½   teaspoon oregano
    Salt and freshly ground pepper to taste

Pour oil into 3-quart microproof casserole.
Add eggplant, onion, and garlic. Stir well,
cover, and microcook on high 6 minutes.
Add squash and green pepper and stir.
Combine tomatoes, parsley, basil, oregano,
salt, and pepper and stir into casserole.
Re-cover and microcook on high about
15 minutes or until vegetables are
tender, stirring twice.

6 to 8 servings

DILLED CUCUMBER BATONS

3   large cucumbers
¼   cup butter
¼   cup dry sherry
    Salt and freshly ground pepper to taste
2   tablespoons all-purpose flour
1   cup half-and-half
1   tablespoon lemon juice
1   egg yolk
3   tablespoons chopped fresh dill

Peel cucumbers, cut in half, and scoop out seeds. Cut into 2 x ¼-inch sticks. Place butter and sherry in 2-quart microproof baking dish. Cover loosely and microcook on high 2 minutes. Add cucumbers, salt, and pepper. Stir well, re-cover, and microcook on high 6 minutes, stirring once. Remove cucumbers with slotted spoon and keep warm. Place 2 tablespoons cooking liquid in 4-cup glass measure. Add flour and stir to make smooth paste. Stir in remainder of cooking liquid slowly. Combine half-and-half, lemon juice, and egg yolk in small bowl and beat until blended. Stir into glass measure slowly. Add dill. Microcook on high 3 minutes, stirring once. Return cucumbers to baking dish, pour sauce over, and stir. Re-cover and microcook on 50% power 4 minutes, stirring once.

6 servings

Desserts to Remember

BRANDIED PECAN PIE

¼ cup sweet butter
1 cup dark corn syrup
3 eggs, beaten
½ cup superfine sugar
5 tablespoons brandy, divided
1½ cups pecan halves
1 9-inch baked pastry shell in microproof
   pie plate
1 cup heavy cream
2 tablespoons confectioners sugar
¼ cup chopped pecans to decorate

Place butter in 4-cup glass measure and
microcook on high 2½ minutes or until
melted. Stir in corn syrup, eggs, superfine
sugar, and 4 tablespoons brandy. Arrange
pecan halves in pastry shell. Pour corn
syrup mixture over pecans slowly.
Microcook at 50% power 14 minutes or
until center is set. Whip cream until soft
peaks form. Add confectioners sugar and
remaining 1 tablespoon brandy. Beat
until firm. Serve pie warm or cold,
topped with whipped cream and
decorated with chopped pecans.

6 to 8 servings

Sauces and Other Treats

PRALINE SYRUP

½   cup firmly packed light brown sugar
½   cup granulated sugar
2   tablespoons light corn syrup
1   tablespoon sweet butter
½   cup half-and-half
½   cup coarsely chopped pecans
1-2 tablespoons brandy

Place brown sugar, granulated sugar, corn syrup, butter, and 1 tablespoon water in 4-cup glass measure. Microcook on high 3 minutes, stirring once. Add half-and-half and beat until well blended. Microcook on high 6 minutes, stirring every 2 minutes. Let stand 2 minutes. Stir in nuts and brandy. Serve warm or at room temperature over ice cream or cake. Refrigerate leftover syrup and reheat at 50% power about 2 minutes.

About 1⅓ cups

BERRY TOPPING

1   package (10 or 12 ounces) frozen berries
¼   cup orange juice
2   tablespoons cornstarch
⅓   cup sugar

1   tablespoon lemon juice
2   tablespoons brandy

Place berries in microproof bowl. Cover loosely and microcook on high 3 minutes. Press through strainer. Place orange juice in small bowl and stir in cornstarch. Add to strained berries with sugar and lemon juice and stir to blend. Cover and microcook on high 3 to 5 minutes or until sauce is thickened, stirring once. Stir in brandy. Serve warm or cold over ice cream or cake.

About 1⅓ cups

GLAZED WALNUTS

2   cups walnut halves
¾   cup sugar

Grease baking sheet. Combine walnuts, sugar, and ¼ cup water in medium-size microproof bowl. Microcook on high 8 to 8½ minutes or until sugar has caramelized, stirring several times. Spread on prepared baking sheet. Cool completely and store in airtight container.

About 2 cups

COATED CHOCOLATE TRUFFLES

12 ounces (12 squares) semisweet
    chocolate
4 egg yolks
10 tablespoons (5 ounces) sweet butter,
    at room temperature
3 tablespoons brandy
3 tablespoons Kahlúa
3 tablespoons Curaçao

To coat Truffles:

> Equal amounts of unsweetened cocoa
> and confectioners sugar sifted together
> Finely chopped nuts
> Chocolate sprinkles

Break up chocolate and place in 2-quart
microproof bowl. Microcook on high 2½
minutes or just until melted, stirring
once. Set aside to cool, stirring every few
minutes. Beat in egg yolks, 1 at a time,
beating well after each addition. Microcook on high 30 seconds. Stir in butter, 1
tablespoon at a time. Beat about 6
minutes or until light and fluffy. Divide
mixture into 3 bowls. Add brandy to 1
portion, Kahlúa to second portion, and
Curaçao to third portion. Stir well. Cover
bowls and refrigerate until well chilled.

Roll candy into ¾-inch balls and coat balls in cocoa-sugar mixture, chopped nuts, or sprinkles. Place in miniature paper cups and store in refrigerator or cool place.

About 4½ dozen

SAUCE MOUTARDE

2   tablespoons butter
2   tablespoons all-purpose flour
1   cup half-and-half
1   cup (4 ounces) grated sharp Cheddar cheese
2   tablespoons Dijon-style mustard
    Salt and freshly ground pepper to taste

Place butter in 4-cup glass measure and microcook on high 1 minute or until melted. Add flour and stir well. Microcook on high 45 seconds. Add half-and-half gradually, stirring constantly. Microcook on high 2½ minutes, stirring once. Add cheese and stir well. Microcook on high 30 seconds or until cheese is completely melted. Stir in mustard, salt, and pepper. Serve with vegetables, meat, fish, or poultry.

About 1½ cups

QUICK BARBECUE SAUCE

1   cup ketchup
¼   cup Dijon-style mustard
¼   cup dark molasses
¼   cup vinegar
1   clove garlic, minced
¼   cup firmly packed brown sugar
1   tablespoon Worcestershire sauce
       Salt and freshly ground pepper to taste

Stir ketchup, mustard, molasses, vinegar, and garlic in 4-cup glass measure until well blended. Add brown sugar, Worcestershire, salt, and pepper, and stir well. Cover loosely and microcook on high about 5 minutes, stirring once.

About 2 cups

ORANGE GLAZE FOR BAKED HAM

1   can (6 ounces) frozen orange juice
       concentrate, undiluted and thawed
½   cup Dijon-style mustard
1   tablespoon cornstarch
1   cup light corn syrup

Place orange juice and mustard in 1-quart microproof bowl and stir until blended.

Microcook on high 1 minute. Dissolve cornstarch in 2 tablespoons water. Add to orange-mustard mixture and stir well. Stir in corn syrup. Microcook on high 3½ minutes, or until glaze is thickened, stirring twice. Spoon over scored ham about 25 minutes before ham is finished baking and baste ham with glaze 2 or 3 times.

About 2 cups

PEACHY-GINGER CONSERVE

2   pounds firm peaches, peeled and chopped (about 3 cups)
2   tablespoons finely diced candied ginger
2   tablespoons lemon juice
1   teaspoon grated orange peel
1   box (1¾ ounces) fruit pectin
1   cup sugar
½   cup fruit-flavored liqueur
1   cup coarsely chopped nuts

Place peaches, candied ginger, lemon juice, orange peel, and fruit pectin in 3-quart microproof bowl. Stir gently, cover, and microcook on high 6 minutes, stirring once. Add sugar and stir. Re-cover and microcook on high 6 minutes, stirring once. Skim off foam. Add liqueur and nuts and stir gently. Set aside to cool. Store in covered containers in refrigerator. Serve warm over ice cream or with ham, chicken, or pork.

About 5 cups

TIPSY BLUEBERRY JAM

3   cups blueberries
1   tablespoon lemon juice
1   box (1¾ ounces) fruit pectin
2½   cups sugar
3   tablespoons brandy

Rinse and drain blueberries. Line baking sheet with waxed paper. Place berries on prepared baking sheet and crush. Spoon into large microproof bowl. Stir in lemon juice and fruit pectin. Cover loosely and microcook on high about 10 minutes or until berries come to a full boil, stirring twice. Add sugar and stir well. Re-cover and microcook on high about 5 minutes or until mixture comes to a full boil again, stirring twice. Boil 1 minute. Let stand 1 minute and stir in brandy. Set aside to cool. Store in covered containers in refrigerator.

About 4 cups

MUSHROOM-TOMATO SAUCE

3   tablespoons olive oil
½   pound mushrooms, sliced
2   cloves garlic, minced
1   cup chopped onion
1   cup chopped green pepper
1   cup chopped celery
1   can (28 ounces) stewed tomatoes,
     chopped
2   cups beef bouillon
1   can (6 ounces) tomato paste
¼   cup chopped fresh parsley
     Salt and freshly ground pepper to taste

Place oil, mushrooms, garlic, onion, green pepper, and celery in 4-quart microproof casserole. Cover and micro-cook on high 10 minutes, stirring once. Add tomatoes, beef bouillon, tomato paste, parsley, salt, and pepper. Stir well, re-cover, and microcook on high 15 minutes or until sauce is thickened, stirring twice. Serve with pasta, fish, chicken, or meat.

About 9 cups

Note: Place unused portion in air-tight containers and store in freezer. Defrost in microwave oven at 30% power. Reheat at 70% power.

INDEX

Copyright © 1988
Peter Pauper Press, Inc.
ISBN 0-88088-437-1
Library of Congress No. 88-60660
Printed in the United States of America

½ teaspoon cinnamon
1 firm banana, sliced
¼ cup chopped walnuts (optional)

Place apples, peaches, pears, and cherries in microproof casserole and set aside. Stir sugar, cornstarch, sherry, and orange juice in 4-cup glass measure until well combined. Cover and microcook on high 2 minutes, stirring after 1 minute. Stir in lemon peel and cinnamon. Pour over fruit and stir gently to coat. Cover and microcook on high 6 minutes, stirring after 3 minutes. Add banana, re-cover, and microcook on high 2 minutes or until fruit is tender. Spoon into serving dishes and sprinkle with chopped nuts, if desired. Serve warm or chilled.

4 to 6 servings

BAKED APPLES SUPREME

6 firm cooking apples
  Lemon juice
6 tablespoons marmalade, divided
4 tablespoons chopped pecans
4 tablespoons chopped raisins
2 tablespoons honey
1 tablespoon finely chopped candied ginger

1   teaspoon grated orange peel
½   teaspoon cinnamon
⅛   teaspoon ground clove
3   tablespoons Curaçao
3   tablespoons orange juice

Core apples to within ½ inch of bottom.
Peel 2 inches of skin from around top of
apples. Brush inside of apples and peeled
portion with lemon juice to prevent
browning. Combine 3 tablespoons
marmalade, pecans, raisins, honey, ginger,
orange peel, cinnamon, nutmeg, and
clove in small bowl. Mix well and spoon
into apple cavities. Place apples, filled
ends up, in microproof baking dish that
will hold apples firmly upright. Combine
remaining 3 tablespoons marmalade,
Curaçao, and orange juice in small bowl.
Stir well and spoon over apples. Cover
loosely and microcook on high 10 to 12
minutes or until apples are tender,
basting apples and rotating dish half turn
after 5 minutes. Place apples in serving
dishes and spoon sauce over. Serve warm
or chilled.
6 servings

Note: Cooking time will vary depending
on size of apples and on whether you
prefer firm or soft baked apples.